MAX notes®

WITHDRAWN

Jane Austen's

Pride and Prejudice

Text by
William Blanchard
(M.A., Hunter College)
Department of English
Gorton High School
Yonkers, New York

Illustrations by
Richard Fortunato

R·E·A *Research & Education Association*

Dr. M. Fogiel, Director

MAXnotes® for
PRIDE AND PREJUDICE

Printed in the United States of America

Library of Congress Control Number 2001098528

International Standard Book Number 0-87891-042-5

MAXnotes® is a registered trademark of
Research & Education Association, Piscataway, New Jersey 08854

What **MAXnotes®** *Will Do for You*

This book is intended to help you absorb the essential contents and features of Austen's *Pride and Prejudice* and to help you gain a thorough understanding of the work. Our book has been designed to do this more quickly and effectively than any other study guide.

For best results, this **MAXnotes** book should be used as a companion to the actual work, not instead of it. The interaction between the two will greatly benefit you.

To help you in your studies, this book presents the most up-to-date interpretations of every section of the actual work, followed by questions and fully explained answers that will enable you to analyze the material critically. The questions also will help you to test your understanding of the work and will prepare you for discussions and exams.

Meaningful illustrations are included to further enhance your understanding and enjoyment of the literary work. The illustrations are designed to place you into the mood and spirit of the work's settings.

The **MAXnotes** also include summaries, character lists, explanations of plot, and section-by-section analyses. A biography of the author and discussion of the work's historical context will help you put this literary piece into the proper framework of what is taking place.

The use of this study guide will save you the hours of preparation time that would ordinarily be required to arrive at a complete grasp of this work of literature. You will be well-prepared for classroom discussions, homework, and exams. The guidelines that are included for writing papers and reports on various topics will prepare you for any added work which may be assigned.

The **MAXnotes** will take your grades "to the max."

Dr. Max Fogiel
Program Director

Contents

> **Each chapter includes List of Characters, Summary, Analysis, Study Questions and Answers, and Suggested Essay Topics.**

MAXnotes® are simply the best – but don't just take our word for it...

"... I have told every bookstore in the area to carry your MAXnotes. They are the only notes I recommend to my students. There is no comparison between MAXnotes and all other notes ..."
    – High School Teacher & Reading Specialist,
    Arlington High School, Arlington, MA

"... I discovered the MAXnotes when a friend loaned me her copy of the *MAXnotes for Romeo and Juliet*. The book really helped me understand the story. Please send me a list of stores in my area that carry the MAXnotes. I would like to use more of them ..."
    – Student, San Marino, CA

"... The two MAXnotes titles that I have used have been very, very useful in helping me understand the subject matter reviewed. Thank you for creating the MAXnotes series ..."
    – Student, Morrisville, PA

A Glance at Some of the Characters

Elizabeth Bennet

Fitzwilliam Darcy

Mr. Bennet

Jane Bennet

George Wickham

Mr. Collins

Charles Bingley

*Lady Catherine
de Bourgh*

SECTION ONE

Introduction

The Life and Work of Jane Austen

Jane Austen, the daughter of an English clergyman, was born in 1775 at her father's Hampshire Vicarage in South Central England. Austen had six brothers and one sister. Austen and her sister, Cassandra, were inseparable. After several attempts to find an appropriate boarding school, they were schooled at home. Their father taught his own children and several who boarded with the family. This education was by extensive reading of the classics. Both sisters were pretty and popular, and they enjoyed most of the social amenities portrayed in Austen's novels.

By the time she was in her mid-twenties, Jane's brothers, two of whom later became admirals, had careers and families of their own. After the father's death in 1805, the family lived temporarily in Southhampton before finally settling in Chawton.

A lively and affectionate family circle and a network of friends provided a stimulated context for her writing. It was the world of landed gentry and the country clergy that she used in her novels.

In the six novels published between 1811 and 1817, Austen revealed the possibilities of domestic literature. Her concentration on personality and character and the tensions between her heroines and their society make her works more closely related to the modern world than to the traditions of the eighteenth century. This modernity, together with the wit, realism, and timelessness of her prose style, helps to explain her continuing appeal to twentieth century readers.

Northanger Abbey, a satire on the romances, was sold for ten pounds in 1803, but as it was not published, was bought back by members of the family. It did not appear in print until after Austen's death.

Although her friends knew of her authorship, she received little recognition in her lifetime. She was quite aware of her special excellences and limitations, and often compared her style to that of a miniaturist painter. She ridiculed the silly, the affected, and the stupid, ranging in her satire from early, light portraiture to later, more scornful exposures.

Austen published several minor works and five major novels: *Sense and Sensibility* (1811), *Pride and Prejudice* (1813), *Mansfield Park* (1814), *Emma* (1816), and posthumously, a collection of *Persuasion* and *Northanger Abbey* (1818). Other minor works included *Juenilia*, the novel, *Lady Susan*, and the fragments: *The Watsons* and *Sandition*. Her name never appeared on her title pages, therefore, she received little recognition until after her death in 1817.

Her comedies of manners depict the self-contained world of provincial ladies and gentlemen, and most of her works revolved around the delicate business of providing proper husbands and wives for marriageable offspring of the middle class. She is best remembered for her lively interplays of character, her meticulous care to style and plot, a sense of comic irony, and her moral firmness. The overall substance of this novel concerns a small section of society locked into a timeless present in which little will change. The people involved are fixed, and the routines and social rituals are predetermined. Money is a problem when it is short. Successful courtships lead to satisfactory marriages. For the first two volumes of the book, Mr. Darcy and Elizabeth Bennet are pre-judging and re-judging. It is a drama of insight that acts by revision and sees things as they really are and not what was presumed.

There is a whole vocabulary connected with the processes of decision, conviction, and opinion. People's varied and unstable judgments are exposed and analyzed. Opinions are constantly changing as characters' behaviors appear in a different light. The need to be aware of the difference between appearance and reality is made clear throughout the novel.

Austen writes about what she knows. Therefore, great areas of human experience are never mentioned. The male characters are not finely drawn. In contrast, the female characters are strong and stand out as intelligent and complex individuals. Extreme passions are avoided. This is demonstrated when Elizabeth accepts Darcy's second proposal. She says, "My sentiments have undergone such a material change as to make me receive with gratitude and pleasure your present assurances." There seem to be many important topics which Austen avoided.

Her greatest talents were her subtle insight into character and her precise dialogue. Each character's speech is appropriate. Collins is pompous, Mr. Bennet is cynical and sarcastic, Elizabeth is forthright and honest, Lydia is frothy and giddy, and Darcy is sensitive and sure of himself.

Although Romanticism was at its peak during Austen's life, she rejected this movement. She adhered more closely to the neo-classic style, and to its discipline, devoid of passion. Her style emphasizes plots that turn like gears on the intricacies of character interaction. Her work is often satiric but underlined with moral purport. She seemed to observe human conduct with an amused and good-humored consciousness.

She once compared her writing style to that of a painter whose subjects are miniatures. This is particularly true of her immaculate attention to detail. She was a perfectionist, and re-wrote most of her novels at least twice.

Jane Austen died at the height of her creative potential at the age of 42. Researchers have suggested the cause to be either Addison's disease or tuberculosis. She spent the last weeks of her life in Winchester, Hampshire in South England and is buried in the cathedral there.

She gradually developed a following in England in the late 1800s, but became even more popular in America. Today, she is regarded as one of the great masters of the English novel.

Historical Background

Austen's fiction reveals little awareness of the political and economic turmoil that pervaded Europe during her lifetime. Wars, such as the Napoleonic Wars, did not affect her middle-class upbringing. The lower classes were recruited, and the upper class purchased commissions and became gentleman officers who enjoyed social prestige.

During Austen's life, the countryside was fragmented into semi-isolated agricultural villages and provincial settlements. London, the only metropolis, was the center of commerce and the arts. Austen had exposure to all three of these areas, and her insights into this society are often reflected in her novels. She was born during the beginning of the Industrial Revolution. Great social unrest was spawned from miserable conditions in factories, and widespread unemployment resulted. The middle classes adopted a laissez-faire attitude. They soon developed methods to mobilize and discipline labor for factory employment. Parliamentary acts established the institutional basis for efficient city, government, and municipal services. Urban police, compulsory education, and government inspection of factories, schools, and poorhouses evolved.

English life was increasingly regulated by central rather than local authority. The working classes, with improved educational opportunities, were raised to a new level of respectability.

During the time that Napoleon was transforming Europe, Jane Austen composed a novel in which the most important events are the fact that a man changes his manners and a young lady changes her mind. Soldiers do appear, but in a secondary role, as fixations of young frivolous women. In one case this even presents an elopement.

Master List of Characters

Elizabeth Bennet—*The proud and witty heroine of the story.*

Fitzwilliam Darcy—*The rich and arrogant man who is enamored with Elizabeth and eventually has her fall in love with him.*

Mr. Bennet—*The dry and somewhat negligent father of Jane, Elizabeth, Mary, Kitty, and Lydia.*

Mrs. Bennet—*The muddle-headed and unrealistic mother of Jane, Elizabeth, Mary, Kitty, and Lydia.*

Jane Bennet—*The eldest of the Bennet daughters, she is mild-mannered and restrained.*

Mary Bennet—*The frivolous and pompous third daughter.*

Lydia Bennet—*The youngest daughter, spoiled by her mother, flighty (an "airhead").*

Catherine (Kitty) Bennet—*The man-crazy daughter. She is similar to Lydia, but sullen and moody.*

George Wickham—*The handsome, unprincipled officer who has a grudge against Darcy.*

Charles Bingley—*Darcy's close friend, the suitor who falls in love with Jane.*

Caroline Bingley—*Charles' cold and indulgent sister. She is enamored with Mr. Darcy.*

Colonel Fitzwilliam—*Darcy's mild-mannered cousin. He is attracted to Elizabeth, but she rejects him.*

Lady Catherine de Bourgh—*Darcy's pretentious, saucy aunt.*

Miss de Bourgh—*Lady Catherine's unsavory daughter.*

Mr. Collins—*Mr. Bennet's cousin. He will inherit Longbourn after Bennet's death as Bennet has no son.*

Georgiana Darcy—*Darcy's timid but well-meaning sister.*

Sir William and Lady Lucas—*The Bennets' neighbors. Parents of Charlotte.*

Charlotte Lucas—*Elizabeth's accommodating and intelligent friend. She marries Mr. Collins for money, much to Elizabeth's dismay.*

Mr. and Mrs. Hurst—*Bingley's conceited sister and his lazy brother-in-law.*

Mr. and Mrs. Gardiner—*Mrs. Bennet's well-educated and intelligent brother and her sister-in-law.*

Mrs. Annesley—*Georgiana's elderly governess.*

Mrs. Reynolds—*Darcy's housekeeper at Pemberley who speaks highly of him.*

Miss Jenkinson—*Tutor of Miss de Bourgh.*

Mrs. Forster—*The wife of an army colonel and a friend of Lydia's who invites her to Brighton.*

Mrs. Hill—*The Bennets' housekeeper.*

Summary of the Novel

Mr. and Mrs. Bennet are intent on having their five daughters marry above their middle-class station. A rich, single man, Charles Bingley rents an estate, Netherfield, nearby. Mrs. Bennet pushes her husband to immediately introduce himself and form an acquaintance. He obliges reluctantly. At a ball, all the Bennets are introduced to the Bingley party. Everyone likes the courteous Mr. Bingley, but his close friend, Fitzwilliam Darcy, is thought to be too arrogant and filled with unconcealed pride and vanity. He won't dance with anyone outside of his own group or deign to speak with them. He states, within Elizabeth Bennet's hearing, that "she is tolerable, but not handsome enough to tempt me."

Mr. Bingley's affection for Jane develops quickly, to the concern of his sisters and Mr. Darcy. They can't tolerate her lower status, and are embarrassed by her family's manners and actions. Mr. Darcy, in spite of his better wisdom, becomes infatuated with Elizabeth. He is drawn to her uncensored wit and fine eyes. Miss Bingley's jealous criticisms of her do nothing to lessen his admiration. Miss Bingley has made plans to entrap him for herself, but they seem blocked.

Caroline Bingley invites Jane to Netherfield. While she is en route, in the rain, Jane catches a severe cold. She is forced to stay at the estate and be treated by a local apothecary. Mrs. Bennet is delighted, because this puts Jane in proximity with Mr. Bingley and his wealth. Jane becomes more ill, and her sister Elizabeth goes to Netherfield to nurse her. The concern for her sister and strength of character appeal to Mr. Darcy, but he is afraid of his infatuation with someone who is economically inferior. The Bennet sisters' departure after six days relieves nearly everyone.

Mr. Bennet's estate, Longbourn, is entailed (by law bequeathed) to Mr. Collins, a clergyman and cousin. This is because he has no son; thus, his property will go after his death to Collins as the nearest male relative. Mr. Bennet receives an inane letter from Collins, apologizing for the entail, and hinting at the possibility of marriage with one of the Bennet daughters. He arranges for a fortnight stay at Longbourn, where his officious stupidity delights Mr. Bennet's keen satiric sense, repels Elizabeth, and endears him to the vacuous Mrs. Bennet.

Mr. Bennet can't wait for him to depart and soon tires of his praise of his patron, Lady Catherine de Bourgh. He sends his cousin on an errand to Meryton with his daughters. There, they meet George Wickham, a handsome and personable military officer. Elizabeth is intrigued when Wickham and Darcy, who obviously know each other, meet on the street and both seem uncomfortable. At a ball, soon after, Wickham tells his life story to Elizabeth. He states that Darcy disobeyed his own father's will out of resentment. (Wickham was a ward of Darcy's father and had been promised revenue for a clergyman's position.) Wickham's story makes Darcy look cruel and self-indulgent. Elizabeth buys this account, because she has pre-determined, negative views of Mr. Darcy's arrogance and pride.

Elizabeth becomes infatuated with the charming Wickham, as do her younger sisters. She resents his absence from the ball thrown by Mr. Bingley at Netherfield. She attributes his lack of attendance to a dispute between Wickham and Darcy, because Wickham has persuaded her of Darcy's bad character. She annoys Darcy by bringing up the subject, and is puzzled by his persistence in approaching her, as she does not know of his attraction. Elizabeth is mortified by her family's behavior that evening. Mrs. Bennet loudly proclaims the merits of a match between Jane and Mr. Bingley. Mary, her sister, bores everyone with her mediocre piano playing. Mr. Collins, her cousin, gracelessly proposes marriage, and she is further embarrassed. He wants a marriage of convenience, and she wants no part of it. She tries to convince him that her refusal is earnest. The support of her father makes Collins see the truth.

The Bingley party leaves Netherfield for London, and Caroline Bingley writes to Jane to inform her that they won't return until winter. She hints in her letter that Mr. Bingley intends to court Georgiana Darcy. This is a match that has been determined for years between the families.

Elizabeth rightly discerns that Bingley's sisters and friend are trying to keep him from the Bennets. Her family is not prominent enough for their aspirations.

Mr. Collins, rejected by Elizabeth, is consoled by Charlotte Lucas, her best friend. To Elizabeth's great surprise and astonishment, Charlotte plots to marry Mr. Collins, "from the pure and disinterested desire of an establishment." She had always considered herself plain and almost an old maid, so she snaps at a chance to be a respectable lady of society. He proposes, they marry, and they leave for their residence near Rosings. Elizabeth later accepts Charlotte's invitation to visit her in her new establishment. Elizabeth is gratified that Charlotte has taken charge, choosing not to react to her husband's stupidity or her patron's insolent behavior. Lady Catherine de Bourgh is a tyrannical despot. She tells everybody what to do, and is not to be contradicted. She plans to unite the family estates by marrying her daughter to Mr. Darcy, who is due to arrive at Easter.

Darcy continues to court Elizabeth. He seeks her companionship, but says little. One night, he declares his love and proposes. He is discourteous, and stresses his family's superiority. Elizabeth is as angry as she is astonished. His seeming pride is unbearable to her, and she adamantly refuses his declaration and derides him. She accuses him of breaking up Jane and Bingley, and ruining young Mr. Wickham's reputation. Darcy acknowledges both charges without seeming remorse or explanation, and leaves her with a cold, indifferent attitude.

The next morning, Darcy finds Elizabeth on one of her walks. He delivers a letter, which tries to answer her reproaches. Darcy intervened in Bingley's romance because he wanted him to marry a wealthy person, and he was not convinced that Jane was truly in love with him. Jane's placid manner never convinced him that there was any deep emotion between them. He went on to add that the Bennet family left a lot to be desired. Mrs. Bennet was vacuous, Mr. Bennet, indifferent and unequivocally negligent, and the two younger daughters were flirtatious and empty-headed. No criticism was leveled at either Jane or Elizabeth. He revealed that Wickham was a man without principle, and had presented his case falsely.

Her former prejudice was now quite jarred, and she had to contemplate the probability of this being true.

Elizabeth and her Aunt and Uncle Gardiner set off on a tour. One of their unofficial stops is at Derbyshire, which is her aunt's and Darcy's home county. Since they are in the vicinity of Pemberley, Darcy's estate, Mrs. Gardiner wants to visit it. Elizabeth has apprehensions, but does not object when she learns the owner is away. She finds Pemberley extremely pleasant. The house is prestigious, and the gardens lavish. Elizabeth muses that if she had been more perceptive and indulgent, this place could have been hers. She hears the housekeeper's glowing description of Darcy as being extremely good-natured and generous to the poor. Darcy unexpectedly appears, a day early, and both he and Elizabeth are embarrassed. Darcy is attentive and gracious and extremely cordial to the unpretentious aunt and uncle. Darcy insists upon Elizabeth meeting his sister, and they call the next day at the inn. The formidable Miss Darcy seems not proud, but shy. She barely is able to carry on a conversation without deference to her brother. There is much affinity between the two. It is not as obvious to Elizabeth that Darcy is still in love with her. The Gardiners see this, but await Elizabeth's version. When Mrs. Gardiner and Elizabeth go to Pemberley for a requested return visit, Miss Bingley tries in vain to insult Elizabeth in her presence and behind her back. She fails completely to work her will on Darcy.

In the midst of her happiness, Elizabeth receives two letters from her sister Jane. They say that Lydia has eloped with Wickham. The pair left Brighton for London and are not presumably married. Elizabeth fears that her sister is permanently disgraced, and that her own re-discovered love for Darcy can never result in marriage. She and the Gardiners leave for home as fast as they can make preparations.

The eloped pair is elusive for several days. Mr. Bennet went after them, but returns home unfulfilled. Mr. Gardiner, who took the matter into his own hands, writes and states that they have been found. He adds that Lydia has agreed to a quick marriage. All of this has been arranged by Darcy. He works secretly to pay off Wickham's gambling debts and ensure a suitable dowry. Mrs.

Bennet is ecstatic about this development. Mr. Bennet, Elizabeth, and Jane are sure that Mr. Gardiner must have paid out a tidy sum to get Lydia married officially and save the family name. Little do they realize that it was Darcy's work.

Mr. Darcy confronted Wickham, bribed him and offered a commission in the army if he would marry Lydia. He did this because of his love for Elizabeth, and because of his sense of blame for Wickham's irresponsibility.

Lydia and Wickham visit Longbourn as a married couple. Elizabeth inadvertently learns of Darcy's involvement in the marriage when Lydia passes on a confidence. She gets the complete story when she writes to Mrs. Gardiner.

Bingley returns to Netherfield and falls in love with Jane again. After a while, he proposes. She accepts. Mrs. Bennet's joy is lessened by the appearance of Darcy, whom she has always distrusted.

Lady Catherine de Bourgh arrives at Longbourn, after hearing a rumor that Darcy is enraptured with Elizabeth. She ridicules Elizabeth and demands her to reject a proposal from Darcy. Elizabeth's answer is reserved. Lady Catherine speaks with Darcy. This only lets Darcy acknowledge that Elizabeth has had a change of heart, and he renews his proposal to her. This time it is met with a positive attitude.

Estimated Reading Time

Fifteen hours should be allowed for the study of *Pride and Prejudice*. The chapters are grouped into sections. The chapters are short, but they should be read closely to capture nuances of plot and characterization. After reading each section, the student should answer all study questions to insure understanding and comprehension. The essay questions are guide-lines to be used, if needed.

Pride and Prejudice Volume One

Chapter 1

New Characters:

Mr. Bennet: *The sarcastic, indifferent father*

Mrs. Bennet: *The foolish and unrestrained mother*

Summary

Mr. and Mrs. Bennet are in their country home, and Mrs. Bennet informs her husband that a neighboring country estate has been rented by a young, wealthy, single gentleman named Bingley.

She insists that as soon as the young man settles in, Mr. Bennet must go visit him.

She already has made up her mind to snare him as the husband of one of her five eligible daughters.

Although Mr. Bennet teases his wife by saying all the daughters are silly and ignorant, he agrees to send Bingley a note telling him that, if he desires any of their daughters, it should be his favorite, Lizzy. Mr. Bennet favors Lizzy because he feels she is more intelligent than his other daughters.

They banter, and Mrs. Bennet again reminds him that he must go calling in person. Then, she complains of her nerves, and Mr. Bennet teases her more.

Analysis

The opening sentence of this novel immediately catches one's attention: "It is a truth universally acknowledged, that a man in possession of a good fortune must be in want of a wife." It sets the ironic tone that implies that the novel will deal with universal truths. The latter part of the sentence relates to a common social situation, that a woman without a fortune is in need of a husband with one.

In the first chapter, Austen is dealing with only a small section of society. She calls it her "inch of ivory" (one piano key in relationship to the whole). It is a tiny, personal portrayal, but is significant in its relationship to the whole of society. The novel manipulates social relationships in a limited culture, and deals with them in minute detail.

There is a great contrast between Mr. and Mrs. Bennet. Mrs. Bennet is effervescent and serious, while Mr. Bennet is reserved and sarcastic. He enjoys teasing her. Austen ends the chapter with her descriptions of their different personalities.

Study Questions

1. Where does the opening scene take place?

2. What does Mrs. Bennet want her husband to do?

3. Why does Mrs. Bennet seem excited?

4. What does Mrs. Bennet consider to be her mission in life?

5. Why does Mr. Bennet favor Lizzy?

6. Who does Mrs. Bennet say will probably visit Mr. Bingley first?

7. How much money does Mr. Bingley earn annually?

8. What is meant by the word "let" in this sentence?

   "Netherfield Park is let at last."

9. What does Mrs. Bennet say a woman with five grown daughters should give up?

10. How many years have the Bennets been married?

Answers

1. It takes place in the country home of Mr. and Mrs. Bennet.

2. She wants him to be among the first to visit their new neighbor, Mr. Bingley.

3. Mr. Bingley is a single man of wealth. She has five marriageable daughters.

4. The business of her life is to get her daughters married.

5. He thinks Lizzy is smarter than the rest of his daughters.

6. She says Sir William and Lady Lucas will go for the same reason.

7. He earns four or five thousand pounds per year.

8. It means the estate is rented.

9. She feels she should give up thinking of her own beauty.

10. They have been married for 23 years.

Suggested Essay Topics

1. The first title Jane Austen chose for this work was *First Impressions*. What are your first impressions of Mr. and Mrs. Bennet? Compare and contrast them. Illustrate this with dialogue that gives insight into their characters.

2. What examples of humor can be found in the first chapter?

Chapters 2–3

New Characters:

Elizabeth (Lizzy) Bennet: *the second daughter. She is intelligent, pretty, and independent*

Jane Bennet: *the eldest daughter. She is kind and beautiful, but too good-hearted*

Catherine (Kitty) Bennet: *next to the youngest daughter. She's "boy crazy" and frivolous*

Mary Bennet: *the inarticulate third daughter, accomplished in provincial arts*

Lydia Bennet: *the youngest daughter. She is giddy, but is Mrs. Bennet's favorite*

Charlotte Lucas: *Elizabeth's best friend. She is sensible and intelligent but very plain-looking*

Sir William and Lady Lucas: *the neighbors of the Bennets and Charlotte's parents*

Charles Bingley: *the handsome, single gentleman who moves next door. He becomes infatuated with Jane*

Fitzwilliam Darcy: *the proud, handsome aristocratic friend of Bingley*

Summary

Mr. Bennet, without telling his family, has already called upon Mr. Bingley. He shocks the family when he relays this information and teases them. The girls all become inquisitive, and Mrs. Bennet is rapturous. She determines to ask Bingley to dinner in the near future. Mr. Bennet refuses to discuss with his family what Bingley looks or acts like, but a neighbor, Lady Lucas, drops by and gives a very favorable report.

A few days later, Mr. Bingley returns Mr. Bennet's visit, and spends some time with him in his library. All the girls spy on him from an upper window, but are not introduced.

He finally meets the Bennet sisters at a ball at Meryton. He is attracted by Jane's beauty and good nature, and dances two dances with her. Jane is equally interested in him. Another person in Bingley's party, the even wealthier Mr. Darcy, attracts everyone's attention. However, his arrogance and coldness make him seem too proud. Mr. Bingley, on the other hand, pleases everyone with his warmth, charm, and fine manners.

The Bennets return from the ball, and Mrs. Bennet is all aflutter. She tries to explain what transpired to a very indifferent husband.

Analysis

Chapter 2 deals with events that are significant in provincial society. The arrival of an eligible man is always important for social and economic reasons.

The third chapter introduces the first of a series of balls in the book. We get our first look at Mr. Bingley and Mr. Darcy. Both are handsome and captivating, but their personalities are totally opposite. Bingley is outgoing and warm, and enchants everyone. Darcy is cool and reserved, and his sharp opinions turn people off.

The first contact between Darcy and Elizabeth is made at the ball when Bingley asks Darcy to dance with her. Darcy's superiority rings through when he remarks that Lizzy is not handsome enough for him. Bingley states that all the girls are handsome. Darcy insists that only Jane is beautiful.

Austen does not present the typical romance where the two main characters fall in love at first sight. In other novels, the hero is perfect and competent, and the heroine is admiring and captivating. Here, we see a heroine who is intelligent and fiercely independent, and a hero who has human frailties. Both Darcy and Elizabeth are characterized by Austen as strong-willed individuals who are not afraid to express their feelings. There is an instant magnetism that attracts them to each other. Yet one can sense that there are going to be clashes of will, and strong emotions will be exposed.

Study Questions

1. How does Mr. Bennet tease his family?
2. What annoying habit does Kitty have?
3. How does Mrs. Bennet show favoritism to Lydia?
4. Why did Bingley turn down the first invitation to dinner?
5. Who came back from London with Bingley?
6. What are the first impressions of most women of Darcy?
7. Who does Bingley find attractive?
8. Why does Elizabeth sit down for two dances?
9. Who overhears Darcy's speech to Bingley? How does she react?
10. What most impresses Mrs. Bennet about Bingley's sisters?

Answers

1. He doesn't tell them right away that he has already called upon Mr. Bingley.
2. Kitty has an annoying cough.
3. She tells Lydia that she will probably get the first dance with Bingley.
4. He had to go to London to bring his relatives back.
5. He brought back his two sisters, his brother-in-law, and Mr. Darcy.
6. They find him to be handsome, but exceedingly vain and cold.
7. He dances two dances with Jane, and describes her to Darcy as the most beautiful creature he has ever seen.
8. There are more women at the ball than eligible men, and some are more popular than others.
9. Elizabeth overhears his arrogant speech, and forms an immediate dislike.
10. She says they dress elegantly and expensively, and are charming.

Suggested Essay Topics

1. How does Austen go against the grain of traditional romance stories of the period?

2. What is the biggest stumbling block in the future development of a romance between Jane and Bingley?

3. What is Lizzy's first impression of Mr. Darcy?

4. Quote some samples of dialogue that give you insight into Darcy's character.

Chapters 4–8

New Characters:

Mr. and Mrs. Hurst: *Bingley's "stuck-up" sister and his lazy brother-in-law*

Caroline Bingley: *Bingley's selfish sister, who has aspirations of becoming Mrs. Darcy*

Mr. and Mrs. Phillips: *Mrs. Bennet's sister and brother-in-law. They own a home in Meryton which Lydia and Kitty love to visit because of the nearby officers' quarters*

Summary

Chapter 4 describes the previous ball, and we are presented with the different reactions of Jane and Elizabeth. Then, in contrast, we learn the reactions of Darcy and Bingley. Elizabeth reproaches Jane for being "blind," which is ironic because later she is the one who becomes blind to Darcy's attention. Elizabeth seems to have a very perceptive nature, unless she is personally involved with the individual. Lizzy also chides Jane about being naive, thinking the best of everyone. Jane admits to her sister that she is quite impressed with Bingley. Darcy and Bingley express totally opposite views of the evening. Bingley enjoyed the people and the ball, but Darcy complained that they're common people with little or no beauty or fashion.

Chapter 5 begins with Mrs. Bennet and her daughters visiting the Lucas' home the next day. The women gossip and discuss the men and their manners. All are quite miffed with Darcy's statement that Elizabeth was merely "tolerable." They end in a big discussion of the differences between pride and vanity. He, apparently, is the epitome of both.

Chapter 6 takes place a few weeks after the first ball. Many social occasions have thrown the Bennets, Bingleys, and Darcy together. There is a definite relationship developing between Jane and Charles. Darcy is beginning to become attracted to Elizabeth, because of her quick wit and perceptive analysis. He discusses his new admiration of Miss Bennet with Charles' sister, who immediately sees Elizabeth as a threat to her own happiness.

Chapter 7 deals with the two youngest Bennet daughters, Kitty and Lydia. Their favorite pastime seems to be to walk to their Aunt and Uncle's home, because an army barracks is located nearby. Their incessant chatter about uniforms and officers irks their father into stating that they are two of the silliest girls in the country.

Jane is sent a note inviting her to dine with Bingley's sister, Caroline, that evening. She has to take a horse instead of the coach, and arrives there soaked to the skin after a severe storm unexpectedly develops. Jane becomes seriously ill with a cold, and she stays the night. Her note the next day alarms Lizzy, who walks through the countryside to visit her. She arrives with muddy feet and stockings, and the two Bingley sisters can hardly hold back their disdain. However, Mr. Bingley and Darcy are impressed by her devotion. This impression is strengthened by the way she handles her silly mother and younger sisters when they visit Netherfield while Jane's condition worsens. Elizabeth stays at Netherfield, and helps nurse Jane back to health.

Analysis

"Pride" and "prejudice" are the twin themes of this novel. Both Darcy and Elizabeth possess excessive amounts of each. The supporting characters in this novel are always discussing one or the other of these two characters and their degrees of these two qualities.

Each individual character's speech indicates something of his/her personality. Mary, the plain daughter, uses polysyllabic words and elaborate, contrived sentences. She tries to make a discourse of every speech. She ends up being pedantic and boring.

Elizabeth is forthright, terse and witty. She often speaks before she thoroughly thinks about what she is saying, and intimidates or aggravates those around her.

Chapter 6 presents several views about marriage. Both Jane and Elizabeth wish for love first and position second. Charlotte wants a conventional marriage, based on practicality. Catherine and Lydia dream of getting a man in uniform.

At another ball, Mr. Darcy approaches Elizabeth for a dance, and she refuses him. He becomes more attracted to her. She, in turn, is puzzled by his interest and becomes intrigued with his motives.

Chapter 7 shows how important it is that the Bennet girls marry well. Mr. Bennet's property is specifically willed to a male heir. He has no sons, so it must go to a cousin, Mr. Collins.

While Elizabeth is staying with the Bingleys, they display their social hypocrisy. They fawn over Jane, yet talk about her behind her back. They describe her family connections as low. Miss Bingley flatters Darcy constantly. Elizabeth teases him with sharp questions.

Study Questions

1. How does Jane describe Bingley to Elizabeth?
2. What does Elizabeth say Jane never sees?
3. What did Charlotte overhear at the ball?
4. What did Miss Bingley and Mrs. Hurst think of Mrs. Bennet and the younger daughters?
5. At the second ball, what does Darcy do that irritates Elizabeth?
6. What is an entailment?
7. What happens to Jane when she visits Bingley's sisters?
8. How do the Bingley sisters react to Elizabeth's appearance when she arrives at Netherfield?

9. What is the name of Darcy's estate?

10. Who is Mr. Jones and why was he sent for?

Answers

1. She says he is sensible, good humored, lively, and has fine manners.

2. She says Jane never sees people's faults.

3. She overheard Bingley describe Jane as the prettiest woman in the room.

4. They thought the mother was intolerable and the younger daughters were not worth talking to.

5. He deliberately listened in on a conversation she had with Colonel Forster.

6. Entailment is a legal term that means a property is bequeathed to a given person (in this case, a male heir).

7. Jane caught a severe cold in the rain and had to remain at Netherfield because she was bedridden.

8. She is muddy and wet, and they find her indelicate and rough.

9. Its name is Pemberley.

10. Mr. Jones is a druggist, and he is asked to bring medicine for Jane.

Suggested Essay Topics

1. Often we misjudge character when we first meet individuals. Give examples of the first impressions that Elizabeth and Darcy form that are incorrect.

2. Mary is the forgotten character in this novel. What references can you find that define her character? How does she differ from Elizabeth or Jane?

3. Austen has an opinion on the difference between pride and vanity. How does it agree or disagree with yours? Cite examples.

Chapters 9–12

Summary

Chapter 9 reveals the difference between Elizabeth and her mother. Elizabeth always displays proper social upbringing, but her mother is oblivious to what is right and proper.

After Elizabeth sends for them by note, Mrs. Bennet and the two youngest girls come to visit Jane. The druggist arrives at about the same time, and announces that Jane is too ill to travel. Several heated conversations take place between Elizabeth and Darcy. Her honesty and opinions begin to infatuate him.

Chapters 10 and 11 convey how Misses Bingley and Hurst interact with the sisters Jane and Elizabeth during Jane's recuperation. Both the Bingley sisters are sarcastic and back-biting when they are out of earshot.

Jane recovers, and she and Elizabeth return home. Mrs. Bennet is not pleased. She had hoped the illness would continue so that closer proximity would have endeared Jane more to Bingley. Their homecoming is welcomed only by Mr. Bennet, who obviously missed Elizabeth and Jane.

Analysis

Darcy and Elizabeth display a continuing relationship permeated with misunderstandings. When he asks her to dance at another ball, she refuses. She believes he sees her to be frivolous and immature. Darcy admits his attraction to her, but is restrained by her lack of social position which he considers an insurmountable obstacle.

In Chapter 11, Darcy says that every person has a defect in character that makes him blind to the goodness of others. Elizabeth answers that his defect is to hate everybody. Darcy countermands with "and yours is a willful ploy to misunderstand them." Both show they have a defect, because of either pride or prejudice, and they need to surmount it.

In Chapter 12, Darcy realizes his love for Elizabeth, and tries to subdue it in action and words. Elizabeth is unaware of this strong emotion. She can always analyze people's feelings, but not when they affect her personally.

Study Questions

1. How does Mrs. Bennet describe Charlotte?

2. What does Miss Bingley ask Charles?

3. To whom does Darcy compose a letter?

4. Why does Miss Bingley get jealous?

5. What weaknesses do Darcy says expose "a strong understanding to ridicule"?

6. What type of entertainment is usually enjoyed after dinner at Netherfield?

7. How long did Jane stay at Netherfield?

8. Why does Darcy hardly speak to Elizabeth on their last day at Netherfield?

9. Why is Mrs. Bennet upset that the two daughters returned so soon?

10. How do the other daughters react to their reunion?

Answers

1. She states that Charlotte is very plain, but a dear friend.

2. She asks him if he is serious about giving a ball.

3. He writes a letter to his sister, Georgiana.

4. She gets jealous, because Darcy is interested in Elizabeth and ignores her.

5. He states that vanity and pride are the two greatest weaknesses in any individual.

6. The usual entertainment is an evening spent in the drawing room.

7. Jane was there for six days.

8. He realizes that she appeals to him, but is acutely aware of her lower social position.

9. She had hoped that they might stay longer, and form a more solid relationship between Jane and Bingley.

10. Mary ignores them, and pursues a study she is engrossed in. Kitty and Lydia "blabber-on" about all the soldiers they've met.

Suggested Essay Topics

1. Why is Darcy afraid of liking Elizabeth too much? What is his concept of what a wife should be?

2. Elizabeth has an "attitude," which her sisters lack. How would you describe it? Is it beneficial to her or does it harm her interactions with others?

3. What other examples of excessive pride or prejudice have you seen? Explain.

Chapters 13–18

New Characters:

William Collins: *Mr. Bennet's cousin, who will inherit Longbourn after Mr. Bennet's death*

Lady Catherine de Bourgh: *Darcy's rich aunt and Mr. Collins' benefactor*

Mr. George Wickham: *the handsome, young soldier who has a grudge against Darcy*

Summary

Mr. Bennet receives a letter from his cousin, the Reverend Collins, who will one day inherit Longbourn. Mr. Bennet makes fun of his writing style and pomposity, and makes snide remarks about him to his family. Collins is planning a fortnight visit with them. He informs Mr. Bennet that he is looking for a proper wife, now that he has been assigned a parish post. If he should happen to select one of the Bennet daughters, it would help him feel less guilty about becoming the heir to Longbourn. Elizabeth questions whether this man can be sensible after evaluating his letter. Again, she shows her ability to see through other people's motives.

Mr. Collins arrives promptly. He is a tall, portly man of 25, and given to pompous speech and manners. He looks at the young ladies in the manner of one who is buying livestock. Every piece of furniture is eyed and evaluated as if it were already his. He is attracted to Jane, but informed that she has a suitor, he settles on Elizabeth. His speech shows how he feels indebted to his sponsor, Lady Catherine. The glowing praise he heaps on her makes her seem saintly.

All the sisters except Mary accompany Mr. Collins to Meryton to visit their relatives, the Phillips. On the way, they run into one of Lydia's soldier friends, who introduces them to a new officer, Mr. Wickham. He's handsome, has good bearing, and is extremely personable. Mr. Bingley and Darcy appear, and immediately there are hostile looks exchanged between Darcy and Wickham. Elizabeth is acutely aware of their distress. The Phillips entertain the party. During their visit, Wickham explains to Elizabeth the reasons behind his animosity to Darcy. They were brought up together since infancy, as Wickham's father was once employed by Darcy's father. The elder Darcy was supposed to bequeath money to support Wickham in a career as a reverend, Elizabeth is told. Now, Wickham blames Darcy for cutting him out of the will, and for his loss of a valuable profession. Elizabeth is shocked and disgusted with Darcy, and believes every detail of Wickham's tale. She thinks Darcy is cruel. Wickham also informs Elizabeth that Lady Catherine de Bourgh and Lady Anne Darcy are sisters. Young Miss de Bourgh has been selected as the perfect wife for Mr. Darcy, because the match would unite the two estates. Wickham derides Lady de Bourgh, and speaks of how proud Darcy's young sister is.

In Chapter 17, Mr. Bingley drops by personally to deliver invitations to his Netherfield ball, and they all look forward to it with enthusiasm. Elizabeth is shocked when Collins asks her to reserve the first two dances for him. She then realizes that he has selected her as his intended.

The ball begins in Chapter 18. Wickham does not attend, and Elizabeth is disturbed and blames Darcy. During a dance with him, she brazenly brings up the subject to Darcy. He denies Wickham's version of events, and becomes quite agitated by her inquiries. Miss

Bingley supports Darcy's version of the story, and further confuses Elizabeth. She holds to Wickham's version, and defies Darcy's explanations.

Analysis

Elizabeth seems to be blinded by her preconceived prejudices of Darcy. She totally believes that Wickham is telling the truth, and accepts his story at face value. She has become attracted to Wickham, and secretly relishes when Wickham derides Darcy's sister, aunt, and pride.

Wickham talks about not defaming anyone's character, and then proceeds to do just that. He even goes so far as to state that Darcy is prejudiced against all people. When Elizabeth tells Jane about Wickham's tale, she speaks well of both people, and again finds it difficult that two gentlemen should have such faults.

The ball is not enjoyable to Elizabeth. She angers Darcy, is forced to dance with Collins, and is embarrassed by her mother's effusive manner and her sister Mary's loud singing.

Study Questions

1. How long does Mr. Collins plan to visit?
2. What is the first subject Mrs. Bennet discusses with Collins?
3. How does Collins describe young Miss de Bourgh?
4. What is the name of the de Bourgh estate?
5. How does Lydia embarrass Collins?
6. Which daughter is of first interest to Collins?
7. What did Darcy and Wickham do on first meeting?
8. What job had Wickham's father held?
9. Does Bingley have any knowledge of Wickham?
10. What does Miss Bingley say to Elizabeth at the ball?

Answers

1. He plans to stay two weeks.

2. She brought up the entailment.

3. He describes her as sickly, but one of the most charming and accomplished women he has ever met.

4. The estate is called Rosings Park.

5. When he is reading to them for entertainment, she loudly interrupts his performance by talking of family matters.

6. He is first attracted to Jane's beauty.

7. They both turned red and stared uncivilly at one another.

8. He was once the steward at Darcy's father's estate.

9. He had never met the man until this encounter.

10. She warns her of Wickham's bad character.

Suggested Essay Topics

1. Locate lines in Austen's prose that describe and reflect the character of Collins. What descriptive phrases does she use that show negative qualities?

2. Why does Elizabeth believe Wickham when she carefully analyzes everyone else?

3. More is discussed about pride and prejudice at the ball. Quote these lines and comment on them.

4. What social blunders are committed by the Bennet family at the Netherfield ball?

Chapters 19–23

Summary

Collins requests an audience with Elizabeth after having told Mrs. Bennet that he means to propose. The proposal is clumsy and condescending. Elizabeth refuses to marry someone for a position or for convenience. She expresses her refusal vehemently.

In Chapter 20, she is backed by her father. Her mother says she will never be seen with her again unless she complies. The house is in an uproar when Charlotte Lucas arrives.

Bingley's whole entourage leaves for London for an indefinite time, without even contacting the Bennets, as Jane learns in a letter. Mrs. Bennet's idle boast at the ball of a match between Jane and Bingley determined Miss Bingley to prevent it, and she convinced Bingley that Jane is indifferent and unsuitable. She sends a letter to the distraught Jane that Bingley is planning to court Miss Darcy, and will be absent the whole winter.

By Chapter 22, Collins proposes to Charlotte. Elizabeth is appalled, her mother disconsolate, and Lady and Lord Lucas are ecstatic.

The section ends with Chapter 23's general reflections on what has come before.

Analysis

Elizabeth's refusal of Collins' proposal implies that she will marry only for romantic reasons. This is further supported by her disdain for Charlotte doing just the opposite. Mrs. Bennet wants the marriage, because Elizabeth is the least favorite of her daughters. Collins seems like a good son-in-law to her. She wants all five daughters married, and she is more concerned with position and income than with romance.

In Chapter 21, Elizabeth again runs into Wickham, and he tells her that he chose not to attend the ball. She approves of this action, and conveniently forgets that he had once stated he would not avoid confrontations with Darcy. As before, her prejudice clouds her from reaching realistic conclusions about his character.

Volume One has now been concluded, but there are several loose ends. Charlotte's marriage to Collins will allow Elizabeth to pay her a visit and be near Darcy. Miss Bingley's letter to Jane shows her prejudice, and leaves open several possibilities. Elizabeth has, for once, been mistaken about the character of her close friend, Charlotte. Could she also be mistaken about other conjectures?

Study Questions

1. What is Mr. Collins' first argument to Elizabeth explaining why he should marry?

2. What does Mr. Bennet say to Elizabeth that he will do if she accepts Collins' proposal?

3. What does Wickham say about his absence from the ball?

4. Who sends Jane a letter?

5. Who does the letter imply should receive Mr. Bingley's affections?

6. Who received Mr. Collins' second proposal?

7. Why does Charlotte agree to become married?

8. How does Mrs. Bennet react to Charlotte's marriage plans?

9. How long will Bingley be absent from Netherfield?

10. How does Charlotte's age reflect on her decision to marry?

Answers

1. He says a reverend should marry to set a good example for his parishioners.

2. He tells her that if she accepts, he'll never speak to her again.

3. He tells Elizabeth that he stayed away to avoid a confrontation with Darcy.

4. She receives a letter from Caroline Bingley.

5. Miss Bingley refers to a prior arrangement for Bingley to marry Georgiana Darcy.

6. His second proposal is to Charlotte Lucas.

7. She has no romantic notions, and wishes to have a position in society.

8. She can only dwell on the fact that Charlotte will someday be the mistress of Langbourn.

9. His sister's letter states all winter. This is a period of six months.

10. She is plain, considers herself an old maid in her late twenties, and seeks to be settled in a position.

Suggested Essay Topics

1. How do Elizabeth and Charlotte's views on marriage contrast? Which was more common in the society presented in this novel? Which do you agree with?

2. What devious type of plan prompted the whole Bingley entourage to leave for the winter? Who do you presume is behind this intrigue? Why?

3. Elizabeth, though intelligent, is fallible in her judgments of character. Show by examples where she has been wrong.

4. At this point in the novel, if you had to select a character that you would prefer to have as a friend, who would it be? Explain your choice.

SECTION THREE

Pride and Prejudice Volume Two

Chapters 1-3

New Characters:

Mr. and Mrs. Gardiner: *Mrs. Bennet's sophisticated brother and sister-in-law. Mrs. Gardiner is an intelligent and elegant young woman*

Summary

When the section opens, Mr. Wickham is a frequent guest at the Bennet home, which casts an ever darker shadow over Darcy's reputation.

Mr. and Mrs. Gardiner, Mrs. Bennet's brother and sister-in-law, arrive at Longbourn for the Christmas holidays. They are so unlike Mrs. Bennet, with their cultured manners and refinement, that it is hard to realize they could be related. Mrs. Gardiner is much like Elizabeth, and the two carry on lively discussions. Most of these center around Jane's plight, and she invites Jane back to their home in London. She hopes such a change of scenery will elevate her spirits. Mr. Gardiner is a merchant, so it is almost certain that their circle of friends would not bring her in touch with Bingley. Elizabeth agrees, and says such an aristocrat like Darcy would never let his friends visit a middle-class neighborhood.

The Gardiners like Wickham, but Mrs. Gardiner has some reservations. She warns Elizabeth of an involvement with a person without money or position. Elizabeth realizes she doesn't really love Wickham. When the Gardiners return to London, she writes to Mrs. Gardiner and tells her that Wickham is now pursuing a plain, 20 year old who has just received a large endowment from a deceased relative.

Jane, while in London, writes to Caroline Bingley requesting a meeting. Miss Bingley's reply is very cold and insincere. She states that Bingley knows Jane is in London. Jane begins to feel that Caroline is probably behind her separation from Bingley.

Analysis

The schism between Jane and Bingley seems to widen and Jane is beginning to become aware that there is hypocrisy and deceit in others' motives.

One reason Elizabeth changes her views about Wickham is that after Darcy left the country, Wickham tries to poison the whole community about Darcy's vindictive and evil character. This is contrary to what he had said about defaming anyone's character.

The two new characters of the Gardiners represent new plot developments. Their upbringing and good taste reflect a position in society that neither Mr. nor Mrs. Bennet could ever hope to attain. Mr. Bennet is so cynical that he has no sympathy for anyone. Mrs. Bennet is narrow, uneducated, and sometimes vulgar. The Gardiners are cultured, genteel, and superior.

Mrs. Gardiner is not fooled by Wickham's charm. Her advice to Elizabeth suggests a better understanding of human nature. Elizabeth again shows how she can misjudge an individual's motives. Normally a good judge of character, she has been taken in by Wickham's studied charm and deceitful manner. Maybe her preconceived convictions of Darcy's true character are also incorrect.

Study Questions

1. Who sends Jane a letter from London?

2. What does Elizabeth say to Jane about her feelings toward others?

3. How does Elizabeth describe Mr. Collins?

4. What does Mrs. Gardiner have in common with Wickham?

5. What does Mrs. Gardiner warn Elizabeth about?

6. Who returns from another visit to Hertfordshire?

7. What favor does Charlotte ask of Elizabeth?

8. Who does Jane visit in London?

9. Who does Wickham court?

10. What does Elizabeth confess in her letter to Mrs. Gardiner?

Answers

1. Miss Bingley sends a letter saying that the Bingley clan is settled for the winter in London.

2. She says again that Jane only sees the good qualities of people.

3. She says, "Mr. Collins is a conceited, pompous, narrow-minded, silly man."

4. They both once lived in the same part of Derbyshire, and know many of the same places and people.

5. She warns her about falling in love with someone with no wealth or position.

6. Mr. Collins comes back and stays with the Lucas family because of his impending marriage.

7. She asks her to accompany her father and sister in March for a visit.

8. After sending two letters and receiving no answer, she calls on Caroline Bingley.

9.   He is now seeing a young lady who recently inherited 10,000 pounds.

10. She states that she has never fallen in love with Wickham.

Suggested Essay Topics

1.   Elizabeth once again changes her views on the true character of an individual. Who is it this time and why does she have a change of opinion?

2.   Why does Jane begin to see faults in Miss Bingley? What incidents alter Jane's opinion of her?

3.   How does the introduction of the Gardiners inject new life into the novel?

4.   What are the similarities between Elizabeth and Mrs. Gardiner? How do they differ in personality?

Chapters 4-8

New Characters:

Maria Lucas: *Charlotte's younger sister*

Colonel Fitzwilliam: *a handsome, well-bred cousin of Darcy who becomes infatuated with Elizabeth*

Mrs. Jenkinson: *the tutoress of Miss de Bourgh*

Summary

Mrs. Gardiner and Elizabeth discuss marriage, Wickham, and money. When they stop for a night in London, Elizabeth is happy that Jane looks better and is enjoying her change of scenery.

Elizabeth, Charlotte's father, and her sister, Maria, visit the parsonage for a fortnight, as they had planned earlier.

At the parsonage, Mr. Collins effusively praises his patroness, and tries to show Elizabeth what she missed by her refusal of his proposal. Elizabeth finds Lady Catherine to be rude, artificial, and condescending. The daughter receives Elizabeth's pity for being reclusive.

During this visit, Darcy and his cousin, Colonel Fitzwilliam, arrive. Darcy is again attracted to Elizabeth, as is Fitzwilliam. Lady Catherine almost compels Elizabeth to play the piano for them at one of the requested dinner invitations, and then complains to Darcy about her style and lack of finesse. Darcy was attentive and enjoyed her performance.

Analysis

Elizabeth's arrival at the Collins parsonage is the essence of Chapters 4 and 5. She reaffirms her distaste for Collins, pities Charlotte's position, and forms a decisive opinion that Lady de Bourgh is not a nice person. The woman is belligerent, domineering, outspoken, and condescending. She allows no one to have conflicting views, and looks down her nose at those she considers to be socially inferior. Her treatment of her young daughter explains why the poor child is so reticent.

A meeting with Darcy, who arrives to visit his aunt, rekindles old feelings. The emergence of Fitzwilliam offers new hope of a future relationship. All the other visitors to Lady de Bourgh's estate feel cowed by her, but Elizabeth is not, and so earns her animosity. Elizabeth doesn't allow her inferior social position to countermand good judgment. She presents herself as an independent person, even when there are social consequences.

She, Darcy, and Colonel Fitzwilliam visit his aunt. Elizabeth questions whether he recently saw Jane in London. His reactions indicate that he didn't know she was there, and thus, Bingley was probably also unaware.

In Chapter 8, Elizabeth and Fitzwilliam seem to have an immediate rapport. Their conversations are animated, and a mutual attraction is evident. Darcy senses this, and shows signs of being perturbed by it.

At the end of Chapter 8, Darcy's aunt shows almost the same qualities of ill-breeding as Elizabeth's mother. She insults Elizabeth, gives rules and regulations to Charlotte, and tries to evince her superiority in all matters of taste. Darcy is embarrassed, and Elizabeth takes some satisfaction that now both families have displayed examples of bad taste. She accuses Darcy of trying to intimidate her during her piano playing, and misunderstands that he was only enjoying her style. They pass further remarks, and Elizabeth becomes aggressive. Darcy only becomes more enamored of her estimation of her own worth, and of her fierce independence.

Study Questions

1. When Elizabeth visits Heresford, where does she stop over?
2. How far was the journey to Collins' parsonage?
3. What do the Gardiners propose to Elizabeth?
4. Who unexpectedly comes to offer dinner?
5. What is Elizabeth's first impression of Miss de Bourgh?
6. How does Lady de Bourgh assess Elizabeth?
7. What games are played after dinner at the fashionable de Bourgh estate?
8. How old is Elizabeth?
9. Who arrives at the de Bourgh's for a visit?
10. Why is Elizabeth attracted to Colonel Fitzwilliam?

Answers

1. She stops over for a day at the Gardiner's, and meets Jane.
2. It was 24 miles.
3. They ask her to tour the lake region as their guest.
4. Miss de Bourgh arrives in her little carriage and offers a dinner invitation.
5. She is shy and timid.
6. She finds her too disrespectful.
7. They play card games, such as quadrille and casino and a variation of blackjack.
8. Elizabeth declines at first to say.
9. Darcy comes along with his cousin Colonel Fitzwilliam.
10. He is well-mannered, handsome, and attentive.

Suggested Essay Topics

1. How is Elizabeth's pre-judgment of Lady de Bourgh confirmed by their first meeting?

2. How does Darcy again present a wrong impression to Elizabeth?

3. How does Mr. Collins show Elizabeth what she has foregone with her refusal to marry him?

4. Upon meeting Miss de Bourgh, what are your first impressions?

5. How does Darcy's aunt portray as much ill-breeding as Elizabeth's mother? Cite examples.

Chapters 9-12

Summary

Darcy arrives at the door, and finds only Elizabeth at home. They talk briefly. Charlotte suggests later to Elizabeth that he is in love with her. Elizabeth does not accept this as probable, and Charlotte sees it her way.

Elizabeth then meets Darcy more than once on walks through the estate's grounds.

Fitzwilliam admires Elizabeth, but because he is the younger son who will not inherit an estate, the match is improbable. In conversation, he lets slip that Darcy saved a friend from an inconvenient match. This news makes Elizabeth angry, because she supposes the woman in question to be Jane. She stays away from the evening's activities at Rosings, out of spite.

Elizabeth peruses all her letters from Jane and detects a sadness she had not perceived before. Her reserve to Darcy for his complicity makes her avoid his presence, and he calls on her at the parsonage. Darcy shocks her by professing his love for her and asks for her hand in marriage. He confesses that he fought his love for her, because of her family, but that his isn't much better. He feels his proposal is such an honor that she should be elated. She, however, is so incensed at his offer, that she adamantly refuses.

She blames him for the separation of Jane and Bingley, for his treatment of Wickham, and for his arrogance and selfish pride. She hurts him even more when she says his behavior is unlike that of a true gentleman. He leaves her coldly, and she bursts into tears of aggravation when she is alone.

As Elizabeth pursues her regular walk the next morning, Darcy delivers a letter to her and promptly leaves the premises. He admits to his involvement in the separation of Jane from Bingley. He confesses that her family often acts with impropriety, and reveals that Wickham is a cordial, but unprincipled young man. He suggests that Wickham is vengeful and full of greed. Darcy says that he did not deprive Wickham of his parsonage, but instead gave him 3,000 pounds to ensure it. Wickham gambled this away and left debts all over the county. Even more vile, when the money was gone, Wickham tried to elope with the naive Miss Darcy, in hopes of bettering his fortune. Darcy prevented this inconceivable match. If she questions these assertions, he asks her to confide in Fitzwilliam, who can confirm his veracity.

Analysis

Elizabeth, initially, refuses to believe the letter, but after constant re-reading she realizes it is probably the truth. She realizes in a moment of despair that vanity has been her downfall, and she has thoroughly misjudged Darcy. She begins to regret her stubborn misconceptions.

The visits of Darcy to the Collins' residence soon begin to signify to Charlotte that he is enamored of her. The introduction of Fitzwilliam allows her to make a further comparison to Wickham. They both are enamored of her.

When Darcy proposes, Elizabeth hurts him more than ever. She refuses and complains that he behaved in an ungentlemanly manner. The refusal is bad enough for Darcy's pride, but in all ways he has performed as a gentleman. This reproach is worse than if she had slapped him or laughed at him. He is crushed, and cannot understand the accusation. The proposal cuts to Elizabeth's pride, and implies that she is only "presentable" again. Darcy is not believed of his real love for her, and is thought to be only condescending. Elizabeth again is angered for the wrong reasons.

Study Questions

1. Why does Fitzwilliam refrain from marriage?

2. Who does Fitzwilliam remind Elizabeth of?

3. What does Fitzwilliam inform Elizabeth that Darcy has done for Bingley?

4. What is Elizabeth doing just prior to Darcy's proposal?

5. What are the reasons that Darcy feels superior to her?

6. Why does Elizabeth reject his proposal?

7. How does Darcy react to her answer?

8. How does Elizabeth hurt Darcy the most?

9. When Darcy leaves, what does Elizabeth do?

10. When Elizabeth receives Darcy's letter the next day, why does she begin to chastise herself?

Answers

1. He is the youngest son and will not inherit money or an estate.

2. He reminds her of Wickham, but he has a better mind.

3. He has kept Bingley from making an improper marriage.

4. She is re-reading Jane's letters, looking for any evidence of Darcy's intervention.

5. He feels she has a low-class family.

6. She is mortified and angry with his pride and insolence.

7. He walks away in cold disappointment.

8. She charges him with acting in an ungentlemanly manner.

9. She breaks down and cries.

10. She realizes that her own pride and prejudice towards Darcy have made her judge him wrongly.

Suggested Essay Topics

1. Explain the circumstances leading up to this declaration by Elizabeth. "Vanity, not love, has been my foll...till this moment I never knew myself."

2. During the proposal scene, Darcy accuses Elizabeth of pride. She accuses him of prejudice. How is this an ironic reversal of their usual reaction to each other?

3. What did Elizabeth accuse Darcy of that made him write the letter to explain his actions?

Chapters 13-19

New Character:

Mrs. Forster: *the wife of an army colonel, and a friend of Lydia's, who invites her to Brighton*

Summary

While Elizabeth is taking her morning walk, Darcy arrives, gives her a letter, and abruptly leaves. The contents of the letter admit that he kept Bingley from Jane as Elizabeth had charged, but that he did so because Jane's calm nature did not show a deep emotional tie. The second part of the letter goes on to list the improper behavior of members of her family. At first reading, Elizabeth is full of resentment and anger, but she soon realizes that his criticism may be harsh but valid. The third part of the letter details the relationship with Wickham, and how deceitful and dishonorable the man was in his version of their estrangement. On reflection, Elizabeth realizes that she has been wrong in her trust in Wickham and prejudices against Darcy. This knowledge of her own lack of discernment and the dishonor she has done Darcy throws her into a deep depression. She is filled with regret for having acted so blindly, and admits that only now is she beginning to know her own faults.

In the next chapter, Elizabeth and Maria leave the parsonage. Prior to their departure, they receive more unasked-for advice from Lady Catherine, and more pompous civilities from Mr. Collins. He again talks of his social position in another attempt to show her what she missed by her rejection of his proposal. They arrive in London, pick up Jane, and continue their journey home.

When they arrive home, Mrs. Bennet and the younger daughters are all upset, because the military regiment is leaving for nearby Brighton. Elizabeth is secretly glad, because she has no desire to see Wickham. Lydia gets an invitation from a colonel's young wife to summer in Brighton, where the regiment is to be now stationed. She lords it over the other sisters, and Elizabeth sees that Darcy's criticism of her was justified. She tries to convince her father that Lydia is not to be trusted on her own. His denial of responsibility only exposes another family weakness.

Her tour with the Gardiners has been shortened by them, because of business. It will be limited to Derbyshire instead of the lake country. Mrs. Gardiner wants to see Pemberley, the Darcy estate, since she knew it as a young girl. Elizabeth only agrees if they can visit when the lord of the house is not in attendance.

Analysis

After constant re-reading of Darcy's letter, Elizabeth comes to the conclusion that nothing Darcy has ever done was less than honorable and fair. She acknowledges Mr. Wickham was always disloyal. She chastises herself for her wanton prejudice and gullible, head-strong behavior. She now accuses herself of what she once labeled Jane. She calls herself "blind." This crucial insight into her own character increases her self-knowledge and gives hope that she can change and rectify some of the damage she has done. She finally has to acknowledge that Darcy had to overcome several objections to the match before he could propose. She is mortified but realizes her family contributed greatly to ruining Jane's chances with Bingley.

The remainder of Volume Two picks up and re-establishes certain plot elements. Elizabeth must return and begin a new adventure. Jane and Bingley will be re-introduced. Wickham should somehow be made to pay for his abominable behavior.

When she returns, Elizabeth relates to Jane all of her letter's contents, except the reference to Jane and Bingley. When Elizabeth learns the militia is leaving, she decides to keep to herself Wickham's true nature. When Lydia makes plans to go to Brighton, she pleads with her father to disallow the visit. She is afraid of another family incident where there would be a breach of decorum.

The overall subject of this novel is marriage, both as a social, economic institution and as the expression of love. The short discussion of the marriage of Mr. and Mrs. Bennet exposes more faults of both. Elizabeth, aware of this, is determined to marry based on a proper relationship between man and wife.

The second volume concludes with the impending trip to Derbyshire, the area where Darby's estate is located.

Study Questions

1. What fault did Darcy place on Jane that encouraged him to break up the relationship with Bingley?

2. How much money was Wickham given?

3. When his money ran out, who did Wickham try to win over?

4. What did Elizabeth say had been her folly?

5. Who came to visit Elizabeth while she read and re-read Darcy's letter?

6. What does Lady Catherine ask Elizabeth to do?

7. Why do Elizabeth and Maria stop at the Gardiners on their way home?

8. What news does Lydia give Elizabeth about Wickham?

9. Why are Lydia and Kitty so agitated?

10. What does Elizabeth warn her father about?

Answers

1. He said she seemed to express indifference.

2. Wickham was given 3,000 pounds.

3. He tried to court Georgiana Darcy.

4. She said that vanity, not love, had been her folly.

5. Both Darcy and Fitzwilliam called to say good-bye.

6. She asks Elizabeth to write a letter to her mother, and to stay for a longer time.

7. They stop there to pick up Jane before returning home.

8. His newly intended, Mary King, has moved to Liverpool and is safe from him.

9. The militia will be leaving town in two weeks.

10. She warns him against Lydia being on her own, near so many eligible men.

Suggested Essay Topics

1. What is the denouement that takes place in Volume Two? Describe three main events leading up to it.

2. Elizabeth gains some knowledge of herself. Explain.

3. How does Darcy answer Elizabeth's doubts?

4. What actions of Elizabeth's younger sisters justify some of Darcy's accusations?

SECTION FOUR

Pride and Prejudice Volume Three

Chapters 1-5

New Characters:

Mrs. Reynolds: *Darcy's housekeeper at Pemberley who speaks highly of him*

Georgiana Darcy: *Darcy's shy but impeccably-mannered sister*

Mrs. Annesley: *Georgiana's elderly governess*

Summary

On a leisurely journey, the Gardiners and Elizabeth stop in Derbyshire to view Darcy's beautiful estate, Pemberley.

The estate is elegant and tasteful, and the housekeeper is overly enthusiastic with praise of her master's fine manners and honest nature. She mentions that he is often thought of as proud, but she will have none of that, having never seen an occasion where he has evidenced this. Darcy's letter has made a great change in Elizabeth. She feels repentance for wrongly accusing him. She looks at his marvelous estate, and reflects that she could have been mistress of Pemberley, if she had been a better judge of character.

Darcy, who was not expected until the next day, appears while Elizabeth and the Gardiners are surveying his gardens. This causes embarrassment on both parts. As a true gentleman, Darcy treats them with civil manners and respect. Darcy is friendly and attentive, and is impressed with this branch of Elizabeth's family tree. He shocks Elizabeth when he asks if he could have the honor of introducing her to his sister during this visit.

Darcy calls on the party the next day, with Georgiana and Bingley. Georgiana is not in the least proud, as Wickham had defined her. She is extremely shy and well-mannered. It is obvious to the Gardiners that Darcy is still in love with Elizabeth. Her feelings have changed, but they remain private. Bingley is obviously not in love with Georgiana, and he makes several references to Jane in his conversations.

Mrs. Gardiner and Elizabeth return the visit the next day. Caroline Bingley, who is present, resents her visit and makes improper comments about how her family must be reacting to the militia withdrawal from their town. Elizabeth takes all this without an offending reply. On her departure, Caroline tells Darcy that Elizabeth looks worse than on their previous encounter. His reply that she is one of the handsomest women of his acquaintance astounds her.

Darcy is trying to make up his mind to propose for a second time to Elizabeth, just as she receives two letters from Jane. Lydia, while visiting at Brighton, has run off with Wickham (without the advantage of marriage). Jane beseeches Elizabeth to return home, while her father goes after the pair to avenge the family name and seek redress. Jane asks that Mr. Gardiner intervene and go to London to help her father to search for the two. Darcy comes to the inn. When hearing of the current crisis, he believes his own silence about Wickham is partially to blame. Believing he is only intruding on a family affair, he leaves. Elizabeth realizes now for the first time that she loves him. This new family scandal, however, has probably ruined her chances forever. Elizabeth and the Gardiners do exactly as Jane has requested. They pack hurriedly, and are on their way home within an hour's time.

In Chapter 5, Elizabeth assures the Gardiners that Wickham will never marry Lydia, because of the lack of family money. They console her, but she lacks confidence in Lydia's good sense and propriety. A letter to Mrs. Forster, in which Lydia says they are to be married and go to Scotland, doesn't console her. It looks like another family embarrassment is evident.

Back at Longbourn, they find a haggard, over-worked Jane, administering to a hysterical mother. Mr. Bennet is in London, and Mary and Kitty are of no help (although Kitty is assumed to have knowledge of the affair). Lady Lucas arrives to "console" the family. In reality, she wants the latest news of the scandal, and they wish she had stayed home.

Analysis

The visit to Pemberley and the conversation with the housekeeper only reinforce Elizabeth's newly-felt regard for Darcy. She now realizes he is a caring brother, is responsible to his servants, and, instead of being proud as she had judged him to be, he does not boast of his accomplishments.

His appearance at the estate embarrasses both, but Darcy handles it with warmth and gentility, and even inquires about her family. He is genuinely pleased to meet the Gardiners, and is extremely courteous. He invites Mr. Gardiner to go trout fishing on his grounds to serve his visitor's interest. He asks permission to introduce Elizabeth to his sister. She is perplexed by his acts. There seems to have been a change in how they both react to each other. The Gardiners are impressed with his impeccable manners and think highly of him.

Elizabeth was prepared to find Miss Darcy unappealing, because of Wickham's description. She, however, finds her not arrogant and proud, but shy and warm. This, along with another meeting with Caroline Bingley, and her arrogance and obvious jealousy, only endear her more to Darcy. Jane's letters present a new family tragedy. Elizabeth is about to believe that she can begin a courtship with Darcy when she receives two letters from Jane.

Lydia, while in Brighton, has eloped with Wickham. Elizabeth is in a state of shock, and when Darcy calls he believes her to be ill. His concern is tender and warm, and she can't react to this. This new crisis only proves to her that Darcy's concerns about her family were just, and that they were open to criticism. She has done him a great injustice.

Both Darcy and Elizabeth feel equal blame for this new situation. Darcy feels his inaction regarding Wickham earlier has caused the predicament. Elizabeth worries about the disgrace to her family.

Study Questions

1. What does Elizabeth insist upon before her visit to Pemberley?
2. What does Darcy ask of Elizabeth that totally "floors" her?
3. What do the Gardiners perceive about Darcy?
4. How does Caroline Bingley try to insult Elizabeth?
5. Why does Jane send two letters to Elizabeth?
6. How does Darcy react to this family scandal?
7. What is Mr. Gardiner prepared to do?
8. Why is it unlikely that Wickham will marry Lydia?
9. How does Mrs. Bennet react to this new predicament?
10. What does Elizabeth admire about Pemberley?

Answers

1. She wants assurances that Darcy will not be there.
2. He asks to introduce her to his sister.
3. They see he is still in love with Elizabeth.
4. She hints that the Bennet family must be very hurt by the militia's decision to leave their town.
5. One got lost in the mail. Both relate the elopement of Lydia and Wickham.
6. He blames himself for not revealing Wickham's true character.
7. He is prepared to go to London and search for Mr. Bennet. He plans to intercept Bennet before he does something rash.
8. She has no family inheritance and is only 16.
9. She becomes hysterical and bedridden. Jane has to minister to her.
10. Pemberley is beautiful but unpretentious. The furnishings

and gardens are done with exquisite taste and are very natural.

Suggested Essay Topics

1. How does Darcy treat the Gardiners? Is this unlike how he treated Elizabeth's immediate family?

2. Why do you think Darcy brought Bingley with him when he introduced Georgiana to Elizabeth?

3. How does Miss Bingley's reaction to Elizabeth's visit give us more insight into these characters?

4. Why was Lydia's current predicament predictable? What hints did you have this might happen?

5. How are the Bennet parents ineffectual in handling this current situation?

Chapters 6-10

New Character:

Mrs. Hill: *the Bennets' housekeeper*

Summary

Mr. Bennet and Mr. Gardiner have little luck in London. They can't find the pair, but almost everywhere they go they find more evidence of Wickham's low character. He is a gambler and has left a trail of debts behind him. Mr. Bennet returns home and leaves the search to Mr. Gardiner. He confesses that Elizabeth was correct when she warned him about allowing Lydia to go to Brighton. He promises to be more strict with Kitty.

Wickham and Lydia are found. They did not get married, but Mr. Gardiner bribes Wickham to do the right thing by offering to pay his debts and provide them with a yearly stipend. Mr. Bennet agrees, and assumes that Mr. Gardiner must have settled a large amount of his own money on Wickham. Mrs. Hill shows that she is inquisitive and offers help.

Mrs. Bennet recovers quickly from her bed, and starts planning the wedding details, from clothes to what estate nearby will be proper for the newlyweds. She then runs off to spread the news to the Lucas family and other neighbors.

Elizabeth contemplates her own chances of ever being with Darcy again. Even if he would marry into such a disgraced family, would he ever accept Wickham as a brother-in-law? When Gardiner writes again and informs them that Wickham has been assigned a new commission in the north of England, Mrs. Bennet is again distraught. Mr. Bennet says they will never be allowed in his home, but Jane and Elizabeth soon persuade him that this would be a further disgrace to Lydia.

Lydia and her new husband arrive at Longbourn soon after. They are both unashamed and very self-assured. Mrs. Bennet is happy for Lydia, and seems proud of the match. It is obvious to everyone that Lydia is in love, but Wickham displays almost no affection for her. Wickham is as charming as ever, and he tries to win back the good graces of Elizabeth. She meets this with cool reserve. Lydia is as flighty as ever, and she informs them that Mr. Darcy was involved with the wedding arrangements. Darcy paid off all of Wickham's debts, set up his new commission, and arranged for the yearly stipend. It was Darcy who found the errant pair, not Mr. Gardiner, as everyone thought. Elizabeth ponders whether this was done because of his love for her or because he felt responsible for Wickham's actions.

Analysis

The settlement after the elopement is carried out by Darcy without anyone except Lydia and Wickham knowing. Many conflicting factors drove Darcy to straighten out the situation.

Mr. Collins is again shown to be a pompous fool. His letter to the Bennets about the elopement is full of criticism. He gloats about not getting involved with such a family. He advises Mr. Bennet to "throw off" Lydia. He also informed Lady de Bourgh of the incident, with the hopes that she will persuade Darcy to keep away from Elizabeth.

Elizabeth realizes from Mrs. Gardiner's letter that Lydia is enjoying this whole melodrama. She realizes again how shallow Lydia is, and how lacking she is in morality or social consciousness.

Jane and Elizabeth, the only Bennets who are aware of Wickham's past, speculate that Mr. Gardiner must have sacrificed a substantial amount to have convinced Wickham to marry. When Elizabeth finds out that Darcy arranged the deal, she feels indebted to him. She respects his mannerly solution.

The two marriages thus far in the novel have been what each of the brides wanted. Charlotte's was for convenience and Lydia's was for lust. It remains for Jane or Elizabeth to make their choices.

When Lydia mentions that Darcy was at her wedding, Elizabeth writes to Mrs. Gardiner. She suspects that Darcy had involved himself because of his concern for her welfare. Mrs. Gardiner confirms this in a lengthy letter. She writes with glowing praise for his character. Austen again uses letters to explain past events and the exact nature of people's roles in them. These letters always give great insight into a character's true nature. Elizabeth realizes she is indebted to Darcy, and again has some hope of a future.

When Elizabeth and Wickham meet again in Chapter Ten, he knows she is aware of the truth. He takes on a subservient role, fearing that she might reveal his true character.

Study Questions

1. Why did Wickham really leave Meryton with Lydia?

2. What does Mr. Collins say about what should be done to Lydia?

3. When Mr. Bennet returns, what does he tell Kitty?

4. Why are Jane and Elizabeth shocked when Mr. Gardiner tells them about the intended marriage?

5. What is one regret Mr. Bennet has about his failure to plan for the future when he was younger?

6. Why was Wickham shipped to a regiment in the north?

7. How do Lydia's actions after her wedding show her true character?

8. Even though promised to secrecy, Lydia blurts out that another person was involved in her wedding. Who was it?

9. How does Elizabeth seek verification of Darcy's part in these arrangements?

10. What does Elizabeth say to Wickham that ensures that she won't talk of his past?

Answers

1. He had a trail of debts and she was in love with him. He decided to turn a bad situation to his advantage.

2. He advises Mr. Bennet "to throw off your unworthy child, and leave her to reap the fruits of her heinous offence."

3. He tells her that he has learned to be more cautious, and that she will feel the effects of it.

4. They know Wickham's character. The money mentioned in the letter seems not enough to satisfy his greed.

5. He wishes that he had set aside part of his annual income for his children.

6. His debts were paid off at Meryton and it was thought best that he start again elsewhere with a clean slate.

7. She is unashamed, flaunts her ring, and wants everyone to call her Mrs. Wickham.

8. She says that Mr. Darcy took charge of the nuptials and made the arrangements.

9. She sends a letter to Mrs. Gardiner asking for the true facts.

10. She says, "Come, Mr. Wickham we are brother and sister. Do not let us quarrel about the past. In the future I hope we shall be always of one mind."

Suggested Essay Topics

1. What are the conditions set for Wickham to marry Lydia?

2. How does Mr. Collins' letter reveal his true nature? Is he jus-
    tified in his appraisal of the situation or merely being vin-
    dictive?

3. Why did Mr. Darcy become involved in such a messy family
    affair? What do you believe his true motivations to be?

4. How do you think Elizabeth will react when she next sees
    Darcy? How would you react?

5. How has Mrs. Bennet again shown her vulgarity?

6. Letter-writing is one of the basic forms of communication
    in the novel. Why is this literacy technique so effective? How
    would the novel be different if the characters had tele-
    phones?

Chapters 11-15

Summary

Bingley and Darcy arrive at Netherfield. Elizabeth is afraid her
mother's behavior will repel them. Mrs. Bennet's rudeness to Darcy
embarrasses Elizabeth, who owes him more than can be repaid.
Darcy is very reserved.

Jane and Bingley come together again at a dinner at Longbourn. Jane tries to convince Elizabeth that they are only on
friendly terms. Elizabeth is troubled by Darcy's reserve. Darcy returns to London, and Bingley proposes to Jane. This is an unex-
pected event, and Elizabeth speculates about Darcy's involvement
in this recent change of affairs. Jane, however, is enthralled.

Lady Catherine de Bourgh comes to Longbourn to try to break
up what she suspects is a relationship between Elizabeth and Darcy.
She is extremely rude, and insists that Miss de Bourgh has been
promised to Darcy since infancy. She belittles the Bennets' worth,
and chastises Elizabeth for her sharp tongue. Elizabeth is not afraid
of her, and practically tells her to mind her own business. Darcy

will make the choice, Elizabeth says. Lady Catherine leaves very angry. She is on her way to confront Darcy, and Elizabeth fears that he may be persuaded to the de Bourgh view of things.

The impact of Lady Catherine's visit is that Darcy will again propose to Elizabeth. He sees that his aunt is condescending and crude. He is ashamed of her behavior. He realizes that Elizabeth has changed her views toward him, and he will return to propose again.

Analysis

These final chapters are written to resolve the plot and bring all the stories together. We are left now to reflect on the Jane and Bingley marriage, the reversal of Elizabeth and Darcy's relationship, and the reasons for each.

The future marriage of Bingley with Jane will be the first real socially accepted marriage in the novel. It will underscore the incorrectness of the first two marriages, which were made for all the wrong reasons.

We also see the differences between the Elizabeth-Darcy and the Jane-Bingley engagements. Jane and Bingley have been constant in their feelings. Elizabeth and Darcy have both undergone great changes, which made them different and better people. Elizabeth has an inquiring mind. Her liveliness is one of the qualities that wins Darcy to her. She is capable of both complex ideas and impressions, and has a stubborn inflexibility of pre-ordained conclusions. He will not be subordinate to another's will. There lies the challenge. Will she be able to accept another's will?

Elizabeth is a heroine who possesses high moral standards, has strong convictions, and an engrained intuition. This provokes many of the heated dialogues with Darcy. What wins Darcy over to her is her basic sincerity, her honesty in approaching reality, and her ability to speak her mind.

Austen lets readers look into character. She allows us to get into the minds of Elizabeth, Darcy and others, and to intertwine their thoughts and project what they will do next.

Elizabeth's love has deepened, and she has become a more understanding, generous, and emotionally stable person. Darcy

has reached outside his world to offer help and assistance, and has been rewarded for it.

Study Questions

1. Soon after Lydia leaves with her new husband, who returns to town?

2. What does Mrs. Bennet ask her husband to do? What is his answer?

3. Who did Darcy sit next to when he was invited to the Bennets' for dinner?

4. What does Jane tell Elizabeth about the current status of her relationship with Bingley?

5. When Bingley arrives for his second dinner invitation, what surprises the Bennet family?

6. How was it obvious that Mrs. Bennet wanted to leave Bingley and Jane alone?

7. What does Bingley do after the third dinner at the Bennets?

8. How does Lady Catherine shock Elizabeth when she unexpectedly calls at Longbourn?

9. What does Lady Catherine try to get Elizabeth to promise?

10. Why does Collins send Mr. Bennet a letter?

Answers

1. Mr. Bingley is returning to Netherfield to do some hunting.

2. She asks him to attend Bingley as soon as he arrives, and he refuses.

3. Mrs. Bennet placed him next to her, and they were both uncomfortable.

4. She says that they are merely friends again and that it goes no deeper than that.

5. He arrives early, and none of the women are yet dressed for dinner.

6. She kept winking at the girls, and finally took Kitty up to her room. Then, she had Mr. Bennet call Elizabeth into the library so Jane and Bingley could be left alone.

7. He proposes to Jane.

8. She tells Elizabeth that Darcy cannot be hers, because he is promised to Miss de Bourgh.

9. She wants Elizabeth to refuse Darcy if he proposes.

10. He wants Mr. Bennet to warn Elizabeth to stay away from Darcy and the de Bourgh family.

Suggested Essay Topics

1. Mr. Collins and Lady de Bourgh are not nice people. Compare and contrast the ways in which they show this.

2. Who best describes the advantages of a match between Jane and Bingley? Why is this a suitable match?

3. How does Mrs. Bennet again show poor taste and bad manners?

4. How was Darcy instrumental in settling the Wickham affair? Who does Elizabeth learn this from?

5. What does Collins say in this new letter to Mr. Bennet? What does Mr. Bennet mean when he states "For what do we live, but make sport of our neighbors, and laugh at them in our turn?"

Chapters 16-19

Summary

Lady de Bourgh is furious, and she goes to see her nephew. She tries to convince him that his feelings toward Elizabeth are unacceptable. She gives him a full account of how Elizabeth treated her, which Lady de Bourgh felt was insufficiently deferential.

Darcy returns to the Bennets after this visit, and they take a long walk together (more than three miles). In their discussion, Darcy begs her for the truth of how she feels. He states his feelings are the same as they were when he first proposed. Elizabeth admits that her feelings have undergone such a radical change that she now loves him. They become sure of each other at last, and they comment on their troubled relationship. Darcy admits that Elizabeth has freed him from his self-centered vanity by her refusal. He only became enamored of her more. He admires her strong opinions and self-assurance. He admits to having given a brotherly chat to Bingley to boost the attachment to Jane. He proposes to her for the second time, and she readily accepts.

Everyone at Longbourn is shocked. Elizabeth had previously shown nothing but contempt for Darcy. Once they believe that the engagement is true, the family behaves as expected. Mrs. Bennet forgets her earlier qualms, and concentrates on Darcy's wealth. Jane is sincere, and truly happy. Mr. Bennet warns her not to make the same mistake he did. He wants her to marry for love.

When the marriages are finalized, Bingley buys an estate near Pemberley (30 miles away), and they are frequently visited by the Bennets and the Gardiners. Kitty seems to benefit most from this upward mobility. In time, even Lady Caroline condescends to visit her nephew and his new wife.

Wickham and Lydia often entreat their now-rich relatives for handouts, but it is usually to no avail. Georgiana and Elizabeth form as close a bond as if they were sisters, much to the delight of Darcy.

In the end, the daughter, Mary, seems content to remain at home and not have to plan for an eventual marriage. We can assume of course that Kitty will soon meet someone acceptable. All the loose ends have been resolved.

Analysis

These final chapters resolve the plot with infinite care and precision to detail. The reader can marvel at the resolution of all the complications.

Darcy has obviously influenced Bingley in choosing a bride. This again displays the reversal Darcy has undergone. He earlier stated that a person should not be led by his friends. Now, we see how Elizabeth has influenced him to change his mind.

Chapter 16 shows the renewed relationship between Elizabeth and Darcy. They have drastically altered their views since their first meetings. We can expect them to continue to adapt to new challenges.

Elizabeth shows that her love has deepened by awareness of her emotional state. Unlike Jane, who was steadfast, Elizabeth has undergone a metamorphosis. Hers will be the most successful marriage in the entire novel.

Austen's skill is demonstrated by her ability to tie up loose pieces of information about subordinate characters and interweave them. Each character is rounded out and final problems are resolved. She is a master of precise dialogue. This is again demonstrated when Elizabeth confesses to Darcy how grateful she is for his unexplained kindness to her sister, Lydia. His reply, that he did this for her happiness alone, and that her family owes him nothing, shows his true respect and love for her. The beautiful moment with the second proposal is a masterpiece of sentiment and refined taste. It is by far one of the most poignant moments in the novel.

The last four chapters are masterful. Every little detail is ironed out, and intriguing conclusions are accomplished.

Study Questions

1. What does Darcy beg of Elizabeth as they are walking after his aunt's intervention?

2. What do Darcy and Elizabeth both admit?

3. Who are the only people who are not surprised by Elizabeth's engagement to Darcy?

4. How does Mrs. Bennet's reaction to the pairing of Elizabeth and Darcy show more of her shortcomings and shallow character?

5. What does Mr. Bennet warn Elizabeth against?

6. What does Darcy say first attracted him to Elizabeth?

7. What does Elizabeth admit to her father after Darcy's proposal?

8. How does Mr. Bennet's concern differ from his wife's?

9. How does Georgiana accept the marriage?

10. Is Elizabeth able to win over Lady Caroline?

Answers

1. He begs to know her true feelings for him.

2. They admit how much they have changed since their former meetings. Each has influenced the other.

3. The Gardiners always perceived a strong affinity between Darcy and Elizabeth, and are extremely happy with the engagement.

4. She immediately accepts Darcy, because of his financial position, and tries to hide her earlier dislike of him.

5. He tries to tell her not to marry someone only to advance her own status, as he did.

6. He admired her independent nature and outspoken ways.

7. She tells him the truth about Darcy's settlement in the Lydia and Wickham situation, and how he resolved it.

8. He wants her to find an acceptable mate, and she wants her to be financially stable.

9. She is extremely happy with Darcy's choice and they become as close as sisters.

10. She accepts the arrangement and eventually comes to call at Pemberly and seeks a reconciliation.

Suggested Essay Topics

1. How do Darcy and Elizabeth show they have overcome their feelings of pride and prejudice?

2. What is revealing about Mr. Bennet's comment on his own marriage? How does this revelation help explain his character?

3. If you were able to place a microphone in a secluded spot, which conversation would you have liked to record? Why?

4. Good sense brings characters together. How does this affect five of the minor and major characters in this novel?

5. What techniques does Austen use to tie up all loose ends at the climax of the novel?

Sample Analytical Paper Topics

Topic #1

Elizabeth's character is influenced by her relationships with other characters in the novel. Write an essay to show how she changes either in a positive or negative manner due to another's influence.

Outline

I. Thesis Statement: *The role of Elizabeth in* Pride and Prejudice *is developed through the negative and positive influences of Jane, Darcy, and Mrs. Gardiner.*

II. Influences of Jane

    A. Positive influences

        1. She can be trusted for her honesty

        2. She will share sisterly confidences

        3. She possesses a forgiving quality

        4. She evinces the goodness of leading a moral life

    B. Negative influences

        1. She never sees evil in others

        2. She keeps everything emotionally inside

III. Influence of Darcy

A. Positive influences

1. He forces Elizabeth to analyze her feelings

2. He makes Elizabeth grow in self understanding

3. He makes Elizabeth change her emotional state

4. He shows Elizabeth how her own pride and prejudices can be overcome

B. Negative influences

1. He is quick to judge

2. He often seems too proud and vain

3. He is sometimes too reserved in speaking his mind

IV. Influences of Mrs. Gardiner

A. Positive influences

1. She helps Elizabeth analyze her true feelings toward Darcy

2. She provides an opportunity to put Elizabeth and Darcy together

3. She shows by example how intelligence and rational thinking can work out problems

B. Negative influences

1. She is sometimes naive about the Bennet family's lack of social class

2. She is often too impressed by the upper class

V. Conclusion: Jane, Darcy, and Mrs. Gardiner are three major characters who influence Elizabeth.

Topic #2

Austen interjects comedy into many of the novel's more serious moments. How do Mrs. Bennet, Mary, and Mr. Collins bring comic relief to some of the novels dramatic scenes?

Outline

I. Thesis Statement: *The comic sides of Mary, Mrs. Bennet, and Collins enable Austen to lighten some of the more serious moments in the novel.*

II. Mary

    A. How is she portrayed?

        1. She speaks like a textbook

        2. She is always the sister who thinks too much

        3. Her comments have little to do with a given situation

    B. Instances of comic relief

        1. She has opinions about events that she knows little about

        2. She has her nose stuck in a book when serious discussions surround her

III. Mrs. Bennet

    A. Her comic contributions

        1. Her dialogues with her husband are comical and ridiculous

        2. Her social blunders are so many that the reader begins to expect them

        3. She lacks logic

        4. When something goes wrong, she hides behind a fit of "nerves"

IV. Mr. Collins

    A. His character and instances of comic relief

        1. He thinks entirely too well of himself, and speaks with a false humility that is pompous, verbose, and long winded

        2. His proposal to Elizabeth is for all the wrong reasons

        3. He fawns over upper-class women

      4.   His letters are full of self-importance and nonsense

V.   Conclusion: Mary, Mrs. Bennet, and Collins provide comic relief.

Topic #3

    The whole novel revolves around attitudes and reasons for marriage. Write an essay comparing and contrasting the marriages of Charlotte, Lydia, Jane, and Elizabeth.

Outline

I.   Thesis Statement: *The marriages of four of the key characters and their pride and prejudices lead them to represent an era.*

II.   Charlotte's marriage to Collins

    A.   Reasons

        1.   He has a title and an estate

        2.   She is plain and unattractive

        3.   She is 26 and nearly an old maid

        4.   It is for convenience only

III. Lydia's marriage to Wickham

    A.   Reasons

        1.   He is handsome and attractive

        2.   He has a commission in the army

        3.   She is 16 and in love

IV.   Jane's marriage to Bingley

    A.   Reasons

        1.   They both fell in love almost immediately upon meeting

        2.   He has a title and money

        3.   It is upward mobility for her

        4.   They are well-matched

V. Elizabeth's marriage to Darcy

    A. Reasons

        1. They share mutual love and understanding

        2. It is a social coup for Elizabeth

        3. They compliment one another

        4. They share trust and have confidence in each other

VI. Conclusion: The marriages of Charlotte, Lydia, Jane, and Elizabeth reflect typical marriages of that period.

Topic #4

Letter writing is a lost art in the twentieth century. Today, we pick up the phone, or send e-mail messages by computer. Letters were usually written in the first person, and they communicated style, intelligence (or lack of it), and insights into character. Explain how Austen used letters to reveal the innermost thoughts of her characters and to express their personalities.

Outline

I. Thesis Statement: *Letter writing in* Pride and Prejudice *reveals a great deal about Collins, Darcy, and Mrs. Gardiner.*

II. Collins' personality as revealed by his letters

    A. His personality is revealed by

        1. His excessive verbiage

        2. His pompous flattery

        3. His insincere understanding or knowledge

        4. His self-pride

        5. His condemnation of others and self-praise

III. Darcy's personality is reflected in his letters

    A. He shows qualities not expressed verbally

        1. His sincerity

        2. His acknowledgment of faults

        3. His perceptive analysis of others

        4. His lack of guile or trickery

        5. His honest devotion to those he admires

IV. Mrs. Gardiner's personality is revealed in her letters

    A. She is steadfast and intelligent with her perceptions

        1. She has almost a sixth sense about character

        2. She can intelligently come to conclusions regarding social situations

        3. She shows warmth and understanding

        4. She is critical but unbiased

        5. She offers hope and understanding

V. Conclusion: Collins, Darcy, and Mrs. Gardiner reveal their personalities and thoughts by writing letters

Topic #5

Write an essay to show how the first impressions of major characters influence the plot and character relationships in *Pride and Prejudice*.

Outline

I. Thesis Statement: *The first impressions of Darcy, Elizabeth, and Lady de Bourgh affect the plot and structure of* Pride and Prejudice *by their influences on other characters.*

II.   First impressions of Darcy

    A.   Positive influences

        1.   He exhibits good breeding

        2.   He is intelligent

        3.   He has pride in his worth

        4.   He seems loyal to his friends

    B.   Negative influences

        1.   He seems to be vain

        2.   He criticizes those below his social status

        3.   He exhibits indifference

        4.   He has strong opinions

III. First impressions of Elizabeth

    A.   Positive influences

        1.   She is accomplished in provincial society

        2.   She is a master of conversation

        3.   She is witty and well-mannered

        4.   She surpasses all of her sisters in intelligence

    B.   Negative influences

        1.   She is quick to make a judgment of character

        2.   She is sometimes too outspoken

        3.   She can be deceived by charm

        4.   She acts before she thinks out situations

IV.   First impressions of Lady Catherine de Bourgh

    A.   Positive influences

        1.   She is wealthy and aristocratic

        2.   She runs a "tight ship" within her household

    3.   She oversees the care of her timid daughter

    4.   She is knowledgeable of all social amenities

B.   Negative influences

    1.   She wants everything decided in her favor

    2.   She is overpowering and strongly opinionated

    3.   She forms immediate opinions on every subject

    4.   She won't permit others to question her view points.

V.   Conclusion: Elizabeth, Darcy, and Lady Catherine de Bourgh are three major characters whose first impressions influence the development of the plot of *Pride and Prejudice*.

SECTION SIX

Bibliography

Austen, Jane. *Pride and Prejudice*. New York: Penguin Books, 1972.

Columbia Encyclopedia. Bridgwater and Kurtz. New York: Columbia University Press, 1963.

Compton's Interactive Encyclopedia. Version 200 VW. Compton's Media, Inc. 1992.

Wright, Andrew H. *Jane Austen's Novels*. A Study in Structure. London, 1954.

Available at your local bookstore or order directly from us by sending in coupon below.

REA's **Test Preps**
The Best in Test Preparation

- REA "Test Preps" are **far more** comprehensive than any other test preparation series
- Each book contains up to **eight** full-length practice tests based on the most recent exams
- **Every** type of question likely to be given on the exams is included
- Answers are accompanied by **full** and **detailed** explanations

REA publishes over 60 Test Preparation volumes in several series. They include:

Advanced Placement Exams (APs)
Biology
Calculus AB & Calculus BC
Chemistry
Computer Science
English Language & Composition
English Literature & Composition
European History
Government & Politics
Physics
Psychology
Spanish Language
Statistics
United States History

College-Level Examination Program (CLEP)
Analyzing and Interpreting Literature
College Algebra
Freshman College Composition
General Examinations
General Examinations Review
History of the United States I
Human Growth and Development
Introductory Sociology
Principles of Marketing
Spanish

SAT II: Subject Tests
Biology E/M
Chemistry
English Language Proficiency Test
French
German
Literature

SAT II: Subject Tests (cont'd)
Mathematics Level IC, IIC
Physics
Spanish
United States History
Writing

Graduate Record Exams (GREs)
Biology
Chemistry
General
Literature in English
Mathematics
Physics
Psychology

ACT - ACT Assessment

ASVAB - Armed Services Vocational Aptitude Battery

CBEST - California Basic Educational Skills Test

CDL - Commercial Driver License Exam

CLAST - College-Level Academic Skills Test

ELM - Entry Level Mathematics

ExCET - Exam for the Certification of Educators in Texas

FE (EIT) - Fundamentals of Engineering Exam

FE Review - Fundamentals of Engineering Review

GED - High School Equivalency Diploma Exam (U.S. & Canadian editions)

GMAT - Graduate Management Admission Test

LSAT - Law School Admission Test

MAT - Miller Analogies Test

MCAT - Medical College Admission Test

MECT - Massachusetts Educator Certification Tests

MSAT - Multiple Subjects Assessment for Teachers

NJ HSPT- New Jersey High School Proficiency Test

PPST - Pre-Professional Skills Tests

PSAT - Preliminary Scholastic Assessment Test

SAT I - Reasoning Test

SAT I - Quick Study & Review

TASP - Texas Academic Skills Program

TOEFL - Test of English as a Foreign Language

TOEIC - Test of English for International Communication

RESEARCH & EDUCATION ASSOCIATION
61 Ethel Road W. • Piscataway, New Jersey 08854
Phone: (732) 819-8880   **website: www.rea.com**

Please send me more information about your Test Prep books

Name _____

Address _____

City _____ State _____ Zip _____